# GREAT PHOTOGRAPHERS
## OF THE CIVIL WAR

# GREAT PHOTOGRAPHERS OF THE CIVIL WAR

## EVA WEBER

## Brompton

First published in 1994 by
Brompton Books Corp.
15 Sherwood Place
Greenwich, CT 06830
USA

ISBN 1-85841-093-2

Printed in China

PAGE 1: **A studio portrait of a
Union private pictured against
a painted backdrop, n.d.,**
Photographer unknown,
*The Bettmann Archive.*

PAGE 2: **Union artillery park,
Yorktown, Virginia, 1862,**
Brady & Company,
*National Archives.*

RIGHT: **"The Bloodiest Day of
the War." Confederate dead
sprawled along the
Hagerstown Pike, Battle of
Antietam, September 17, 1862,**
Alexander Gardner,
*Library of Congress.*

# CONTENTS

# INTRODUCTION

The opening salvo of the American Civil War was not the shot fired at South Carolina's Fort Sumter on April 12, 1861, nor was the conflict's first photographic plate exposed by Mathew B. Brady, as has long been popularly assumed. On February 8, 1861, during the military build-up around the fort following the secession of six Southern states beginning with Mississippi on January 9, Charleston photographer George S. Cook persuaded the garrison's commander Major Robert Anderson and his officers (including Abner Doubleday, the mythic founder of baseball) to pose for photographs. He immediately sent on the negatives to New York's E. and H. T. Anthony & Company, the nation's largest photographic supply house and leading photographic publisher. In a clever marketing strategy designed to sell these topical pictures, Anthony made up a humorous broadside-style advertisement, in the guise of a battlefield news flash, emblazoned with the headline, "Major Anderson Taken!" It described how "Col. George S. Cook, of the Charleston Photographic Light Artillery . . . heroically penetrated to the presence of Maj. Anderson, and leveling a double-barreled Camera, demanded his unconditional surrender in the name of E. Anthony and the Photographic community."

Despite its jesting tone and commercial aim, the broadside did convey an essential truth: the first pictures of the Civil War were taken by Southern photographers. This is only logical since this first exchange of hostilities took place deep in Confederate territory. When Major Anderson surrendered Fort Sumter to the rebels on April 13, Charleston's Osborn & Durbec were on hand to document the structural damage in a three-plate panorama, and in the following days they produced over 40 stereographic views of the fort and the opposing victorious Confederate batteries across the harbor. Theirs was probably the first and most extensive coverage of a Civil War engagement. Also present was F. K. Houston who, on April 15, captured an intensely moving image for Southerners — that of the new rebel flag fluttering over Fort Sumter's parade ground.

The only other Union stronghold located in the South, Fort Pickens at the entrance to Florida's Pensacola Bay, now became the focus of Confederate military activity. On May 14, 1861, New Orleans photographer J. D. Edwards advertised the availability of 39 views of Pensacola; of Forts Barrancas, McRee and Pickens; of troops from New Orleans, Mississippi and Alabama at drill and in camp; and of the United States fleet. By June 15, woodcut engravings based on these photographs appeared in *Harper's Weekly*, the New York pictorial magazine which was to become a leading disseminator of Civil War visual imagery. Also in the spring of 1861, New Orleans photographer J. W. Petty made the most complete surviving set of pictures of a Confederate unit in the field. His series on the Washington Artillery, later to become famous for their association with the Army of Northern Virginia, was probably photographed as the group mustered before leaving New Orleans.

During the first three months of the war when little occurred in the way of combat, Northern photographers, Brady cameramen among them, recorded scenes of soldiers

LEFT: **The Martins, son and father, shown in Civil War (left) and Revolutionary War uniforms, n.d.,** Photographer unknown, *Confederate Memorial Hall, New Orleans, LA.*

RIGHT: **The Ottawa, Illinois, home of Union Brigadier General W. H. L. Wallace, with his portrait and horse in the foreground, n.d.,** William Bowman, *Chicago Historical Society, Chicago, IL.*

in training in the military camps surrounding Washington, D.C. Finally on July 21 the war's first real battle, Bull Run, took place in Manassas, Virginia, some 25 miles from the nation's capital. This is where Brady, already an internationally celebrated portraitist, created his legend as the pioneering and omnipresent photographer of the Civil War. When hostilities appeared imminent Brady, having obtained the necessary permissions, set out for the front. After a humiliating defeat for the Union, his equipment was damaged as panic-stricken soldiers and civilian spectators retreated in chaos.

On his return to Washington Brady immediately had himself photographed in his disheveled dusty camera technician's coat and straw hat, thereby presenting himself as dauntless adventurer as well as the premier documentarian of war. With this image, Brady demonstrated his genius for public relations by transforming failure into triumph — no matter that the photographs he said he took at Bull Run have never surfaced, and were probably apocryphal.

It is now generally agreed that Brady personally did not take a single Civil War photograph, as his eyesight had become very bad by the late 1850s. Most of the photographs appearing under his name were taken by his corps of camera operators. Success as a portraitist made it possible for him to obtain the financial credit to outfit, supply and pay the salaries of some 20 photographers who covered the war for him. Functioning as an impresario with invaluable connec-

tions in government and the military, Brady made arrangements, issued instructions, probably selected camera positions whenever he was in the field, and added to his ever-increasing archive of Civil War photographs by purchasing, exchanging, and possibly copying without permission the work of other photographers not in his employ.

Even the claim that Brady was a visionary who conceived the grand scheme of photographing the war in its entirety to create an indelible historic document is now in question. Not only did his assistant Alexander Gardner, who may have seen Crimean War photographs in London, England, counter this by insisting the idea came from him, but also news and copies of the early Confederate war photographs had penetrated North, and photographing the war had come to dominate discussions among photographic circles. Whether or not he originated the concept, Brady did possess the enthusiasm, energy, and dedication to follow the project through to the end, and beyond.

Of the four greatest Civil War photographers of all – Alexander Gardner, Timothy O'Sullivan, George Barnard and Andrew J. Russell – the first three worked for Brady at various times, while Russell was the only regular Union Army

BELOW: **The field quarters of photographers of the Army of the Potomac's Engineer Corps, n.d.,**
Photographer unknown,
*Library of Congress.*

RIGHT: **Mathew Brady after the First Battle of Bull Run, July 22, 1861,**
Brady & Company,
*Library of Congress.*

Photo taken
July 22ⁿᵈ
1861

BRADY
The Photographer
returned from
Bull Run

officer assigned full-time to photography. Fine photographs also were taken by other Brady men – James Gibson, David Woodbury, James Gardner, David Knox, John Reekie, Jacob F. Coonley, Thomas C. Roche, William Pywell, and Egbert Guy Fowx among them. (When the photographer of a Brady image remains unidentified, the work's author is now referred to as Brady & Company.)

Numerous other independent cameramen executed Union Army contracts, as did Samuel A. Cooley in South Carolina; or photographed while enlisted in the army, as did Philip Haas of Haas & Peale, who recorded the 1863 siege of Charleston; or followed home-town boys through a series of campaigns, as did Vermont's G. H. Houghton; or memorialized their days as an army of occupation, as did New Hampshire's Henry P. Moore. Fortuitously located cameramen were able to take advantage of circumstances, as did the Tyson brothers at Gettysburg, Royan M. Linn who put a studio atop Tennessee's scenic Lookout Mountain, and San Francisco's Lawrence & Houseworth who detailed the construction of an ironclad ship. And the makers of some of the best pictures are still unknown.

The South could not begin to match this wide-ranging

LEFT: **Lieutenant Colonel Hallewell, 28th Regiment, "His Day's Work Over," Crimean War, 1855,**
Roger Fenton,
*National Army Museum, London, England.*

RIGHT: **Damage caused by the mine in the Chutter Munzil, The Indian Mutiny, 1858,**
Felice Beato,
*National Army Museum, London, England.*

coverage. Despite the pioneering work done by Cook, Osborn & Durbec, and Houston at Fort Sumter, and by Edwards and Petty out of New Orleans, the lack of dependable financial backing and difficulties in obtaining photographic supplies necessarily limited Confederate efforts. Yet unique blocks of work survive: McPherson & Oliver's documentation of the Battle of Mobile Bay, and Andrew D. Lytle's chronicle of life in Baton Rouge under Yankee occupation. The South, nevertheless, is the dominating subject of Civil War photography, even in the far more prolific work of Northern cameramen. As nearly all of the engagements took place within Confederate-held territory, American Civil War photography is in large part a record of the fortifications, towns, rivers, sea coasts, and topography of the South.

Technological advances in photography had made possible its extensive use in documenting the Civil War. The daguerreotype, brought to the United States in 1839 by painter and telegraph inventor Samuel Morse, was a direct and unique image. The wet-plate process, introduced in 1851, involved coating a glass plate with collodion, a sticky fluid that dried rapidly to a transparent film. Sensitized with chemicals, it was exposed in a camera to make a reproduct-

ible negative which had to be developed before the collodion dried. A negative made the mass reproduction of photographs an economically feasible venture.

The difficulties of transporting into the field the necessary bulky and fragile equipment – including cameras of different sizes, heavy glass plates, chemicals, water, developing equipment and dark-room tents – was solved by using specially-outfitted wagons and enlisting the help of assistants. Once the glass plate negatives were developed and coated with a protective film, they were sent back to the studio where multiple photographic prints were made in sunlight by laying the negatives over sensitized paper.

The era's most popular photographs were the 2½ by 4 inch *carte-de-visite* introduced in France in 1854. As many as eight separate exposures could be made on a single glass plate by using a multi-lensed camera. (Enlargements could also be made from these small negatives.) The pictures – often celebrity portraits – were eagerly collected and frequently displayed in special albums. Equally in demand were stereographs, also mounted on cards and usually sold in sets. The three-dimensional illusion of these photographs was produced by two separate views of the same subject

taken from twin lenses separated by about the same distance as between the eyes. These multiple prints from twin- or triple-lensed cameras could be cut apart to be sold as single *cartes-de-visite* or mounted in pairs as stereographs to be examined through special viewers. The small cost and universal distribution of these images made them the mass media of the 19th century.

Photography's first war images were taken by an unknown American daguerreotypist during the Mexican War (1846-48). Of the series of street scenes of Saltillo, Mexico, four depicted U.S. troops. Pictures of the siege of Rome (1849) by S. Lecchi and of the Second Sikh (1848-49) and Second Burma Wars (1852-53) by British military surgeon John McCosh influenced later developments far less than the numerous and widely publicized Crimean War (1853-56) views by the professionally-equipped Roger Fenton, whose somewhat posed work recorded British participation in the militarily inept campaign. Felice Beato's far more disturbing pictures of the Indian Mutiny (1857-58) and China's Opium War (1860) also predated the American chronicle. However, American Civil War photography is unprecedented and unique for the scope of its coverage of varied aspects of the war, for the sheer numbers of cameramen at work, for the raw depiction of war's brutal realities, and for the breadth of distribution of these images to the general public. From 1861 to 1865 some 1500 photographers probably exposed over one million plates, from which at least several hundred thousand images still exist.

In subsequent U.S. military involvements, photographers emphasized the heroic qualities of war while downplaying its negative aspects − voluntarily in the Spanish-American War, and under strict official censorship in World War I, World War II and the Korean War. In Vietnam the uncensored images by photographers critical of the conflict were a powerful force in turning public opinion against the war. During the following decades the U.S. military, having relearned a painful but crucial lesson, once more imposed strict censorship during the Grenada and Panama invasions, and the Gulf War.

Why the shocking Civil War images of the dead at Antietam and Gettysburg did not invite censure is a matter of conjecture. Perhaps the easy answer is that most of the dead portrayed were Confederate and hence could be regarded as propaganda in the campaign to raise Union morale.

LEFT: **Confederate dead gathered for burial, 1862,** Alexander Gardner, *Library of Congress.*

BELOW: **Scenes from the battle of Antietam, October 1862,** A woodcut published in *Harper's Weekly* based on photographs by Alexander Gardner and James Gibson, *American Antiquarian Society, Worcester, MA.*

RIGHT: **Grant and his generals at Massaponax Church, 1864,** A woodcut taken from a photograph by Timothy O'Sullivan which appeared in *Leslie's Illustrated News, Archives and Special Collections Department, Otto G. Richter Library, University of Miami, Coral Gables, FL.*

SCENES ON THE BATTLE-FIELD OF ANTIETAM.—From Photographs by Mr. M. B. Brady.—[See Page 663.]

Though these photographic images could be viewed in public gallery exhibitions and purchased in stereograph and album card sets, the state of printing technology did not allow their reproduction as such in the era's leading pictorial periodicals, *Harper's Weekly* and *Frank Leslie's Illustrated Newspaper*.

Instead, war photographs were reproduced in the form of wood engravings, some of which were relatively true to the originals, while others deleted some details and added others in order to convey a typically sentimental interpretation of events. The Antietam photos appeared as engravings in *Harper's* after only a five-week delay, while a version of the Gettysburg Union dead – O'Sullivan's famous 1863 *Harvest of Death* – was not published in *Harper's* until after the war ended. In this case *Harper's*, a strong supporter

of the Union cause, obviously exercised self-censorship, while its images of emaciated Union prisoners of war served to indict the Confederacy. The numerous sketch artists in the field at times also used photographs as a basis for their more dramatic, dynamic and often less reliable version of events.

This use of photography to sway public opinion was not new. As early as the mid-1840s, abolitionists promoted their anti-slavery cause by issuing a daguerreotype button showing a dark-skinned hand and a light-skinned hand resting on a prayer book. A before-and-after photograph of a freed slave in a Union Army uniform, and the photo of the scarred back of a beaten slave sought to gain sympathy for African-Americans, while encouraging both their enlistment and their acceptance by whites. *Carte-de-visite* portraits and images were sold as well to raise money for war-related

RIGHT: **The spot where Union Major General McPherson, Army of The Tennessee, was killed during the Battle of Atlanta, July 22, 1864,**
George Barnard,
*Special Collections,*
*United States Military Academy*
*Library,*
*West Point, NY.*

LEFT: **An explosion at City Point, Virginia, on August 9, 1864,**
A pencil sketch by Alfred R. Waud used as the basis for an engraving which appeared in *Harper's Weekly* on August 27,
*Library of Congress.*

BELOW LEFT: **Scene of an explosion, City Point, Virginia, August 9, 1864,**
A. J. Russell,
*Library of Congress.*

causes such as the education of former slave children and the support of wounded soldiers, orphaned children and war widows.

The widest publication and distribution of photographs came in the form of numbered series of album cards and stereographs depicting specific events of the war. Alexander Gardner's 1863 *Catalogue of Photographic Incidents of the War*, offered sets such as "Sherman's Expedition to South Carolina," "War in Virginia," "McClellan's Peninsula Campaign," "Hooker's Virginia Campaign," and "Meade's Pennsylvania, Maryland and Virginia Campaign." The eight photographers of these views included Gardner himself, O'Sullivan, Gibson and Barnard. The first to issue such series for sales, as early as 1862, was Brady with his *Brady's Photographic Views of the War, Brady's Album Catalogue,* and *Incidents of the War.*

Mathew Brady (1823-96), whose name was synonymous with Civil War photography for well over a century, earned his reputation as the era's leading daguerreotype portraitist. Born near Saratoga Springs, New York, he opened a New York City studio in 1844. By the late 1850s he owned luxurious establishments in New York and Washington, which catered to the powerful and wealthy, and displayed famous faces from his *Gallery of Illustrious Americans*. Income from the portraiture helped to fund his grand Civil War project, as did seemingly endless financial credit in the form of photo-

graphic supplies from Anthony.

Around November 1862 his Washington gallery manager Alexander Gardner left, followed by other cameramen probably dissatisfied because their photographs were still credited in the press to the Brady name even though they had been copyrighting their own work since May 1862. Moreover, the financially-strapped Brady was slow in paying their wages. Increasing difficulties led Brady to declare bankruptcy in 1868 and again in 1873, while he sought to find a permanent repository to house and preserve his historic collection of Civil War negatives.

The loss of the business acumen and considerable photographic talents of Alexander Gardner (1821-82) was a blow from which Brady never really recovered. Possibly in the place of wages, Gardner took along with him negatives from Antietam, the Peninsular Campaign, First and Second Bull Run, General Pope's Virginia Campaign, and O'Sullivan's South Carolina views. He successfully established his own gallery around the corner, and most of his Brady associates came to work for him as well, including O'Sullivan, James Gibson, William Pywell, John Wood, W. Morris Smith, David Knox, John Reekie and his brother James Gardner.

Born in Paisley, Scotland, Alexander Gardner was a former jeweler, loan manager, an Iowa utopian community organizer and Glasgow newspaper editor, who left behind his own photographic studio when he emigrated to the

United States in 1856. He contacted Brady in New York, was taken on as assistant and two years later became manager of Brady's new Washington gallery. Of the 137 photographic portraits of President Lincoln, Gardner took 37 on seven different occasions – more than any other photographer. In November 1861 he began work for the Union Army, duplicating maps for the U.S. Topographical Engineers, and through the intercession of fellow Scot, Allan Pinkerton, was appointed honorary captain in the Army of the Potomac. In this position he carried out special assignments for the Secret Service. Unrelated to his army work were his powerful views of dead soldiers at Antietam and Gettysburg, and of the ruins of Richmond.

After the war, in 1866, Gardner published the ambitious two-volume *Photographic Sketchbook of the War*, combining text with 100 photographs by himself, O'Sullivan, Barnard, Gibson, James Gardner and his other operatives. In 1867, he began photographing the West for the Kansas Pacific and the Union Pacific Railroads. By the 1870s he was back at his Washington studio photographing Indian treaty

delegates, among others. Undoubtedly his most lasting impact on photographic history came with his sequential documentation of the execution of Lincoln's assassins – the forerunner of modern photojournalism.

Now considered one of the 19th century's finest photographers, Timothy O'Sullivan (1840-82) was one of Gardner's most experienced and productive cameramen. He was born to Irish immigrant parents and raised on Staten Island, New York. By 1860 he had become an apprentice in Brady's New York gallery under the supervision of Gardner, whom he accompanied to Washington when Gardner was named manager of the new Brady gallery there. O'Sullivan, who had traveled with Brady to Bull Run in July 1861, was sent from December to May 1862 to carry out the war's first successful photographic coverage of a campaign – Brigadier General William T. Sherman's attempt to secure bases essential to the Union blockade of shipping in the area of Beaufort, Hilton Head and Port Royal, South Carolina.

There he obtained views of Union regiments at Beaufort, Union graves at Hilton Head, abandoned Confederate posi-

FAR LEFT AND LEFT: **Contraband Jackson and Drummer Jackson, n.d.,** Photographer unknown, *U.S. Army Military History Institute, Carlisle, PA.*

RIGHT: **Members of the 6th Connecticut Regiment outside a "Dagtyps" gallery tent, c.1862-63,** *albumen silverprint,* Henry P. Moore, *New Hampshire Historical Society, Concord, NH.*

tions at Fort Walker and the ruins of Fort Pulaski, Georgia. He returned north to photograph around Manassas in July 1862, before following General John Pope's Virginia Campaign to Warrenton, Culpepper and the crossing of the Rappahannock River, documenting bridges, railroad stations and other scenes, culminating with his coverage of the Cedar Mountain battlefield only a few days after hostilities ended. Present at the Second Battle of Bull Run, he was again forced to fall back to Washington.

Two days after Gettysburg, O'Sullivan was present, along with Gardner and Gibson, to obtain some 60 collaborative photographs of the battlefield and the still-unburied bodies. In May 1864 he began coverage of Grant's Army of the Potomac's Virginia Campaign, photographing the crossing of the Rapidan River, Spotsylvania, Massaponax Church, the North Anna River, Cold Harbor, the James River crossing, Petersburg and Appomatox Courthouse. Many of his photographs were included in Gardner's *Photographic Sketchbook*.

After the war he went West as expeditionary photographer to join the King, and later Wheeler, surveys, with a side trip to Panama in 1879 to record the U.S. Navy's search for a canal route. Finally, in ill health, he returned East to work briefly for the government before dying of tuberculosis at the age of 42.

During his long career in photography, George Barnard (1819-1902) produced images documenting pivotal historic events, as well as artistic views of unique subtlety and sophistication. Born in Coventry, Connecticut, he grew up in central New York state, with time spent living with relatives in Nashville, Tennessee. In 1846 in Oswego, New York, he opened a very successful daguerreotype portrait studio. In the earliest news photo in existence, he captured the Oswego mill fire of July 5, 1853. Active in photographic circles, he sought to elevate photography to the level of the other arts and saw, as well, the importance of preserving early photography. In 1854, he opened another studio in Syracuse. An 1859 New York City trip led to a long association with Brady, and especially Edward Anthony, resulting in an 1860 Cuban trip to produce a scenic stereo series. In 1860-61, Barnard and Jacob F. Coonley (whom he had

trained) made for Anthony *carte-de-visite* negatives of the entire Brady collection.

With the outbreak of war he probably worked for both Brady and Anthony, making portraits, in collaboration with C. O. Bostwick, of Washington military personnel, producing scenic views of the capital's vicinity, photographing Harper's Ferry and covering the Lincoln inauguration. He also witnessed the First Battle of Bull Run but was not able to photograph the battlefield, together with James Gibson, until March 1862 when the rebels drew back. In late June, Barnard documented Yorktown after its capture.

In 1863 he continued to work for Brady, Anthony and Gardner until he was hired, on December 28, 1863, by the Topographical Branch of the Department of Engineers, Army of the Cumberland, in Tennessee. As official photographer for the Military Division of the Mississippi, he duplicated maps, made portraits and produced topographic, fortification and battlefield views around Nashville, Knoxville, Chattanooga and from atop Lookout Mountain.

On September 11, 1864 he was summoned to Atlanta to follow Sherman's March to the Sea, documenting the devastation of Atlanta, Savannah, Charleston and Columbia, South Carolina. Allowed to keep a number of his army negatives, he published a selection in his 1866 *Photographic Views of Sherman's Campaign*. After the war he moved to Charleston, and then in 1871 to Chicago, just in time to document the Great Fire. He spent the rest of the decade in Charleston operating a photographic studio and then "retired" to Rochester, New York, where he worked on new photographic processes with George Eastman. After time spent in Ohio and as an Alabama farmer, he returned to central New York where he spent his last years.

Andrew J. Russell (1830-1902), who worked as a painter and illustrator as well as a cameraman, recognized that his Civil War photographs would teach future generations that "war is a terrible reality." Born in Nunda, New York, he started out as a portrait and landscape painter. The outbreak of war inspired his *Panorama of the War for the Union*, a large painted diorama based on engravings of Brady camp and battlefield scenes. In August 1862 he enlisted as a captain with the 141st New York Infantry Volunteers, and by the fall was assigned as photographer-artist to General Herman

Haupt's U.S. Military Railroad Construction Corps, active in facilitating the movements of the Armies of the Potomac, Virginia and the Rappahannock in the Virginia sector. There he photographed fortifications, buildings, troop-transport equipment, and the erection and dismantling of bridges and roads in order to formulate a historical and practical record of military engineering experiments and procedures. Haupt included with the text of his 1863 instruction manual, *Photographs, Illustrative of Operations in Construction and Transportation*, 82 images by Russell.

In early 1863 he hired former Brady man and Baltimore photographer Egbert Guy Fowx as assistant for three months, paying his $100 monthly salary from his own pocket. Russell's assumption of these expenses and his additional duties as acting quartermaster and ordnance officer of Haupt's unit were carried on with the understanding that Russell could keep all the negatives of the photographs he took for the army. He also accompanied Haupt to battlefields, and recorded scenes of camps, wharves, supply depots, weaponry and fortifications around Belle Plain,

LEFT: **Abandoned Confederate trenches southeast of Atlanta, n.d.,**
George Barnard,
*Library of Congress.*

RIGHT: **Bridge of the East Tennessee and Virginia Railroad crossing the Holston River at Strawberry Plains, near Knoxville, Tennessee, 1863,**
George Barnard,
*Library of Congress.*

BELOW: **Self-portrait of Samuel Cooley and staff, c.1864,**
*U.S. Army Military History Institute, Carlisle, PA.*

Fredericksburg, Alexandria, City Point, Petersburg, the James River, and Richmond under occupation. Beside his official large-plate negatives, he apparently also produced unofficial stereo views to sell to Anthony. After the Civil War had finished, he documented the West for the Union Pacific Railroad and for the King Survey. On his return to New York City, he established a studio and also became an illustrator for *Leslie's* magazine.

Biographical information on many of the lesser-known Union photographers remains sparse. What happened to Alexander Gardner's younger brother James, who worked for him during the war years producing many memorable photographs, is not clear. Possibly he joined the western King survey in 1866, and later may have become partner in the Boston photographic firm of Gilmore & Gardner.

William Pywell (1843-87), whose sister married Timothy O'Sullivan, accompanied Alexander Gardner to Kansas, became official photographer to Colonel David Sloan Stanley's 1873 Yellowstone expedition, and spent his last years in Louisiana as a studio photographer. William Bell (1836-1902) from Liverpool, England, came to the U.S. at an early

age, and in 1860 opened a Philadelphia studio. He served in the military from 1862 to 1869, initially as member of the Pennsylvania Volunteers and then as a photographer for the Army Medical Museum in Washington, where he documented the wounds suffered by soldiers. In the 1870s he served as western expeditionary photographer with the Wheeler survey.

James P. Gibson, whose experience in covering McClellan's Peninsular Campaign made him one of the most accomplished battlefield photographers of his time, assisted Alexander Gardner in making the momentous images of the dead at Gettysburg and Antietam. Many of Gibson's works were listed in Gardner's 1863 catalog. Gibson also collaborated with George Barnard in photographing Manassas, and with John Wood and with David B. Woodbury on the Peninsular Campaign. (Woodbury, who produced many fine images for Brady and Gardner, died of tuberculosis in 1866.) Gibson later became Brady's business associate when, in 1867, he purchased a half interest in Brady's ailing Washington gallery. In 1868, Brady announced that Gibson had mortgaged the gallery and left for Kansas.

LEFT: **Grant and his staff on Lookout Mountain, Chattanooga, Tennessee, after General Joseph Hooker's "Battle Above the Clouds," November 25, 1863,** photographer unknown, *National Archives.*

ABOVE: **Artist James Walker at work on Lookout Mountain, Chattanooga, Tennessee, November 1863,** Photographer unknown, *Chicago Historical Society, Chicago, IL.*

Thomas C. Roche, whose most famous photographs documented Confederate dead at Forts Mahone and Sedgwick after the final Union assault on Petersburg, learned his craft as an amateur in 1858. In 1862 he developed a close relation with Edward Anthony, and was associated with Brady until mid-1864. While working under Quartermaster General Meigs as "Photographer of the Railroad Department," Roche continued to produce large numbers of stereo views for Anthony. In the last months of the war, Meigs assigned Roche first to photograph the structures and *matériel* at the Union supply depot at City Point and then to document the occupied cities of Petersburg and Richmond in Virginia. After the war, Roche continued photographing for Anthony in the far West.

That remarkable work was produced by little-known cameramen is proven by the 1862-63 Hilton Head portfolio of Henry P. Moore of Concord, who followed New Hampshire troops south. From a makeshift "DAGTYPS" gallery he took portraits of soldiers, scenes of camp life and of military installations, as well as exquisite views of Seabrook plantation life on the semi-tropical Edisto Island. Also active in the South Carolina and northern Georgia coastal regions was Samuel A. Cooley who executed contract work for the Union Army from 1861 to 1865. Designating himself "U.S. Photographer, Department of the South" and "Photographer, Tenth Army Corps," he produced for the Quartermaster's Department numerous views of Union occupation forces, government structures, ships and fortifications in Beaufort, Hilton Head and Folly Island, South Carolina, with side trips by his men to the siege of Charleston, Fort Sumter, Savannah and even Jacksonville, Florida. No record exists of his pursuit of photography after the end of the war.

Yet another unique Southern coastal series was produced by Haas & Peale. Philip Haas, a New York photographer who served as a lieutenant in the 1st New York Engineers, collaborated on this portfolio with Washington Peale, a photographer attached to General Gilmore's army in Charleston.

They produced over 40 serially-numbered views of the 1863 siege of Charleston. These medium-format images documented military camps, soldiers and officers on Morris and Folly Islands; the Union batteries aimed at Forts Sumter and Wagner, and gunboats at sea.

An equally high quality distinguished the work of Brattleboro photographer G. H. Houghton, who followed Vermont troops on at least two trips to the Virginia front in 1862 and 1863. The 100-odd large, detailed images which survive were intended for sale back home and cataloged officers and men, camp life, seas of graceful white tents set in panoramic landscapes, drills, weaponry and the army on the move.

Known as "The Photographer of the Confederacy," George S. Cook was born in 1819 in Stratford, Connecticut, and moved to the South as a boy. In 1844 he founded one of the first photographic studios in New Orleans, established studios in other Southern cities and in Charleston in 1849. When Brady traveled to Europe in 1851-52, Cook managed his New York gallery and developed a relationship with the neighboring Anthonys. Throughout the war, Anthony continued to provide Cook with photographic supplies. Many of

Cook's views of soldiers and sites around Charleston were produced under contract for the Confederate Army. He became one of the few to capture scenes of actual battle when, during the 1863 siege of Charleston, he fortuitously photographed a Federal shell exploding inside Fort Sumter; and later he drew fire when he photographed the Union ironclad fleet from a parapet. After the war he continued his portraiture business in the South.

Cook's leading competitor for the title of "Photographer of the Confederacy" was J. D. (Jay Dearborn) Edwards (1831-1900) of New Orleans. Originally from New Hampshire, Edwards arrived in New Orleans around 1857 and made some of the earliest surviving views of the city. He established a portraiture studio, but specialized in outdoor photography. During the Civil War years, he followed Louisiana troops throughout the South. He also acted as a spy for the Confederacy. After the war he settled in Atlanta where he opened a photography studio.

A. D. (Andrew David) Lytle (1834-1917) who documented the war years in Baton Rouge, Louisiana, under Union occupation, was born in Deerfield, Ohio. By 1856 he was working

LEFT: **Mourning Confederate women pass through the ruins of Richmond, 1865,**
Photographer unknown,
*Library of Congress.*

ABOVE: **The ruins of the Nashville and Chattanooga Railroad Bridge, n.d.,**
Photographer unknown,
*Library of Congress.*

Mart'' and documented the Confederate capture of Fort Sumter in more than 40 images, of which few survive. Their partnership itself did not survive the end of the war. J. W. Petty of New Orleans rarely ventured out of his studio after his pioneering 1861 coverage of the Washington Artillery. In Baton Rouge, McPherson & Oliver covered much of the same wartime activity as A. D. Lytle. They completed a series on the Mississippi and the Union naval fleet. The Union Army hired them to document siege trenches, Confederate fortifications and other sites along the Mississippi; and later they photographed Fort Morgan in Alabama for the Union Department of Engineers. Probably their most important contribution was their series on the Battle of Mobile Bay.

When these tumultuous years finally ended in a hard-won peace, the photographic chronicle of the events, faces and places of the past four years was cast aside in the public mind. People wanted no reminder of what they had just been through; they just wanted to forget. Yet the failure at war's end of the photographs, stereographs and war albums to continue to sell did not discourage all photographers. While the military guns may have fallen silent, some photographers continued their shooting – of victory parades, of historic battlefields and of reunions of old soldiers.

as a daguerreotypist in Cincinnati. During the late 1850s he traveled throughout the South as an itinerant photographer, and in 1859 opened the Baton Rouge photography studio he was to operate for the next 50 years. Soon he was busy making portraits of soldiers, and in the following years surveyed the camp life, regimental activities, hospitals and batteries of the Union forces. He made numerous views of warships on the Mississippi and, according to some reports, may have acted as a spy for the Confederate secret service, particularly when Baton Rouge became the staging area for the Union attack on Port Hudson.

Much less is known about other Confederate photographers such as Charleston's Osborn & Durbec – James M. Osborn and F. E. Durbec – who ran a large ''Photographic

# FRIENDS AND ENEMIES

Of the vast numbers of photographs taken during the Civil War years, portraits constituted the major part. Studio photographers in both small towns and large cities flourished as never before, as soldiers leaving for the front had their images recorded for posterity, often many times. With each successive wave of recruitment came additional waves of customers, both soldiers and their loved ones. In the early years when war was regarded as a romantic adventure — as a chance for heroism and glory — other photographers caught up in the war fever abandoned their studios and followed the soldiers into camp, in the hope of multiplying their business. Some set up temporary studios in tents while others occupied the huts (with roofs pierced by skylights) from which they offered portraits at $1 each. Still other itinerant photographers, who lacked the resources for darkroom wagons, carried all their supplies and equipment, including folding darkroom boxes, on horseback. The Army of the Potomac was served by as many as 300 freelance civilian photographers, some of whom followed the army for years.

Two recently introduced photographic processes were exploited by these portraitists — the ambrotype and the tintype. Cheaper, faster and more durable (in the case of the tintype) than the daguerreotype and the paper portrait printed from a collodion glass negative, they were ideal for serving transient customers. Patented in 1854, the ambrotype consisted of a negative image made by the collodion process on a small glass plate which, when placed over a black background, appeared as a positive image. Set into attractive cases like daguerreotypes, ambrotypes were a popular item with soldiers.

The tintype also used the collodion process on a metal sheet painted black or dark brown. Using a multilensed camera, a single sheet could yield four 2½ × 3½ inch tintypes, or as many as 12 to 30 very small images. These were then cut apart with tin shears, and sometimes were hand tinted for greater realism. Requiring no case for protection or viewing, the tintype could be sent through the mail, or carried into battle in uniform pockets. One entrepreneur advertised a specially designed ''Soldier's Belt,'' a modified money belt with separate sections for greenbacks, letters and photographs. Probably of greatest interest, aside from the evocative faces, is the information offered about details of uniforms and weaponry in the portrait of the anonymous common soldier.

The image of the celebrated ''uncommon'' soldier reached a far wider audience. The portraits of war heroes, officers and generals — known to the public from news dispatches — were available in cartes-de-visite eagerly purchased and collected into albums by a citizenry caught up in the mid-19th century cult of personality epitomized by Brady's Gallery of Illustrious Americans. Brady participated by inserting himself into many of the war photographs taken by his men. For a time, Anthony issued some 3600 album cards a day, many of them of military celebrities, at 25¢ each. (Indeed, the concept of the modern photo agency originated with Anthony who commissioned and bought negatives from photographers on both sides of the Mason-Dixon line.) These album cards and other photographs carried a revenue tax, so that those buying them supported the war effort.

Group portraits were big business too. They ranged from formal regimental portraits and more casual assemblages, to distant views of encampments or of men posed around equipment and structures. These uniformed, flag-bearing troops represented national pride, strength, order and common purpose in a disorderly world. The aesthetic quality of some of the images in which soldiers merge picturesquely with landscape or architecture is remarkable. A few of the groups were taken with a darker purpose — some of Gardner's photos were taken to aid the Secret Service in identifying spies.

Camp life was an early subject of war photographers. In May 1861 Barnard and Bostwick surveyed military life at Camp Cameron near Washington, while Anthony soon offered a ''War Scenes'' series by Roche, focusing on Union camp life. Many of these often stiffly-posed images reflect the idea of war as an adventure and the cameraderie of the men. Some included civilians who regularly visited to sample such camp entertainments as band concerts. African-Americans usually were seen in stereotyped roles — as mistreated slaves, fugitives or ''contrabands,'' refugees, servants or laborers — but in portraits as uniformed men were accorded the same dignity as other soldiers. And in the early years the life of prisoners of war did not seem so different from that of regular soldiers. What permeates these static scenes is the aura of marking time and waiting — probably an opportunity to pose for pictures marked a welcome break in the routine.

The immediacy and texture of army life was captured by Russell, Gibson and Edwards who sometimes were able to photograph the soldiers before they could pose. One of the justly most famous Civil War pictures, Russell's image of Union soldiers in a trench just before combat, is one of the few to convey the hardship and tension of a life under fire. It is an anomaly in the pervasively positive portrayal of the Civil War soldier, who usually responded to the cameraman's approach by putting on his best face.

**Confederate Prisoners on Seminary Ridge, Gettysburg, July 1863,**
Brady & Company,
*National Archives.*

LEFT: **A montage of officers of the 1st Virginia Heavy Artillery, Baton Rouge, n.d.,**
A. D. Lytle,
*U.S. Army Military History Institute, Carlisle, PA.*

ABOVE: **Lieutenant Custer (with dog) and fellow officers during General McClellan's Peninsular Campaign, May 1862,**
James Gibson,
*U.S. Military History Institute, Carlisle, PA.*

**Union soldiers entrenched along the West Bank of the Rappahannock River at Fredericksburg, May 1863,**
A. J. Russell,
*National Archives.*

**Union General McClellan's Headquarters Guard, the 93rd New York Volunteer Regiment, at Antietam, September 16, 1862,**
Alexander Gardner,
*U.S. Army Military History Institute, Carlisle, PA.*

**Drying Cotton, Seabrook's Wharf, Edisto Island, South Carolina, 1863,**
Henry P. Moore,
*New Hampshire Historical Society, Concord, NH.*

**Seabrook Plantation, Edisto Island, South Carolina, n.d.,**
Henry P. Moore,
*New Hampshire Historical Society, Concord, NH.*

**Union General Herman Haupt on a makeshift pontoon, March 1863, (detail),**
A. J. Russell,
*Collection of the J. Paul Getty Museum, Malibu, CA.*

**Alfred Waud sketching at Gettysburg, July 1863,**
Timothy O'Sullivan,
*Library of Congress.*

**A fancy group in front of Petersburg (rooster fight), August 1864,**
David Knox,
*Library of Congress.*

**Soldiers bathing in the North Anna River, Virginia, May 25, 1864,**
Timothy O'Sullivan,
*Library of Congress.*

**Ferry Landing on Mason's Island across from Georgetown in Washington, D.C., c.1864,**
George Barnard,
*Library of Congress.*

**Confederate encampment, probably Orleans Cadets, near
Pensacola, Florida, n.d.,**
J. D. Edwards,
*Florida State Archives, Tallahassee, FL.*

**Federal troops in an abandoned rebel camp on Marye's Heights
outside Fredericksburg, Virginia, 1863,**
A. J. Russell,
*Chicago Historical Society, Chicago, IL.*

**Union servants at rest outside a cook tent at Culpepper,
Virginia, November 1863,**
Timothy O'Sullivan,
*Library of Congress.*

**Arlington, Virginia, former residence of General Robert E. Lee,
June 28, 1864,**
A. J. Russell,
*The Bettmann Archive.*

**Johnson's Mill on the Appomattox River near Petersburg, Virginia, May, 1865,**
Timothy O'Sullivan,
*Library of Congress.*

**The 5th Vermont Regiment at Camp Griffin, 1861,**
G. H. Houghton,
*Library of Congress.*

# OFFENSE AND DEFENSE

Combat may well be the essence of war, but in the 1860s it just was not possible to photograph in the heat of battle. The nature of the available photographic technology – the wet-plate process – precluded the taking of instantaneous views of what the public wistfully visualized as glorious feats of gallantry. That aspect of war had to be left to the agile fingers and often fertile imaginations of the sketch-artists who also followed the armies and sent back their drawings to be published as engravings in *Harper's Weekly* and *Leslie's Illustrated*.

Everything about the wet-plate process conspired against its use in the dangerous and rapidly-changing circumstances of combat – the fragile and heavy equipment had to be transported by slow-moving darkroom wagons, and the inescapable requirements of the picture-taking and developing process were an equal deterrent. The photographs could not just be snapped in quick succession and the film then set aside for development later at a safer time and place, as is done today.

Rather, the entire procedure had to be completed with meticulous precision on location with an assistant's help for each individual exposure, usually within the span of some 20 minutes: a glass plate was cleaned and polished, then evenly coated with viscous collodion, then sensitized in the darkroom by submersion for five minutes in a bath of silver nitrate, then drained and inserted in a light-shielding holder, then inserted in the camera and exposed, then returned to the darkroom and removed from the holder, then treated with developing chemicals, rinsed, treated again and well washed in clean water, and finally air dried and coated with a protective film before it was packed away for shipment back to the studio where multiple prints could be made from this laboriously produced negative.

Hence many of the battlefield, artillery battery and trench scenes were taken weeks and even months after the battle. The Manassas meadows of First Bull Run (July 1861) were not surveyed by Barnard and Gibson until March 1862. The timely photographing of the 1861 fall of Fort Sumter by Confederates F. K. Houston and Osborn & Durbec was not surpassed until Antietam and Gettysburg, when Gardner and his men began work within hours. Though it may have been possible to capture conflicts in long-distance views, the black powder employed in battle obscured everything with great clouds of smoke. Gardner's panoramic view of the Antietam battlefield, heralded by some as the only combat picture of the war, is probably not of actual fighting since the artillery is not in use and the smoke seems to be rising from campfires. Cook possibly came closest to an "action" picture with his 1863 view of a shell exploding in Fort Sumter.

Most of the deliberately posed scenes of soldiers next to artillery or guarding fortifications were taken during training exercises, or following the occupation of enemy installations. The marching views usually were taken during drill time or parade. The most realistic photographs of soldiers in action were those of the army on the move, and of men involved in road and bridge construction.

For the Union Army, which ordered great numbers of photographs, the camera had become an invaluable tool for documentation. The army commission which traveled in 1855 to the Crimean War summed up its observations in a report including photographs by Englishman James Robertson. Photographs of battlefields, fortifications, weaponry, bridges and transport came to be used for analysis, strategic planning, illustration of reports, and the instruction of cadets at West Point. In the field the camera routinely was used to duplicate maps, documents, architectural drawings and mechanical plans. In 1862 Gardner used a large-format camera to reproduce maps for the Department of Topographical Engineers, and panoramic photos of topography were essential for map making. The Ordnance Department even used photography to record their tests of the tensile strength of iron. This proved to be a useful aid in the design of larger cannons.

Officers associated with engineering, supply, the medical branch and transport ordered most of the photos. The Head of the Department of Engineers ordered a survey of the construction of fortifications, types and amounts of ordnance, and siege operations. Barnard surveyed Atlanta's trenches and defensive positions for him. Quartermaster General Montgomery Meigs, a talented amateur photographer himself, ordered views of all buildings, warehouses, railroad depots and ships controlled by his branch from Russell, who photographed Arlington cemetery, from Cooley, of Southern coastal installations, from Roche in Virginia, and from Coonley in the western theater.

The Military Medical Department had William Bell document soldiers' wounds. And General Haupt of the U.S. Military Railroad Construction Corps assigned Russell to document the results of his reconstruction and reorganization of the army transport systems, as well as his experiments with innovative boats, bridge trusses and floating docks. Through the agency of spies, images of Federal *matériel* were informative and perhaps discouraging to Confederate strategists.

Haupt who, like the others, used photos as supplements to reports, also sent special presentation sets to other generals for instructive purposes, to political leaders for persuasive purposes and to foreign diplomats to assure them of Union strength and of the "inevitability of its triumph."

**Fort Sumter, 1865,**
George Barnard,
*Library of Congress.*

ABOVE: **The interior of Fort Sedgwick, "Fort Hell," near Petersburg, Virginia, April 1865,**
A. J. Russell,
*National Archives.*

RIGHT: **A Union signal station on Elk Mountain overlooking the battlefield of Antietam, Maryland, October 1862,**
Alexander Gardner,
*Library of Congress.*

**Sherman's troops destroying a section of railroad, Atlanta,
Georgia, 1864,**
George Barnard,
*Library of Congress.*

**At work on military bridge over Chickahominy Creek, Virginia, 1862,**
David Woodbury,
*Chicago Historical Society, Chicago, IL.*

**Mortar "Dictator" in front of
Petersburg, October 1864,**
David Knox,
*National Archives.*

**The hospital and ordnance storeyard, Hilton Head, South Carolina, 1862,**
Henry P. Moore,
*New Hampshire Historical Society, Concord, NH.*

**Union troops and artillery crossing a river, n.d.,**
A. J. Russell,
*Library of Congress.*

**Battery A, 2nd U.S. Artillery, after Battle of Fair Oaks, Virginia,**
**June 1862,**
James Gibson,
*Library of Congress.*

**The steamer *Fulton*, Pensacola navy yard, Florida, 1861,**
J. D. Edwards,
*Southern Historical Collection, Wilson Library, The University of North
Carolina at Chapel Hill, Chapel Hill, NC.*

**The Aquia Creek and
Fredericksburg Railroad
bridge over Potomac Creek,
April 18, 1863,**
A. J. Russell,
*Library of Congress.*

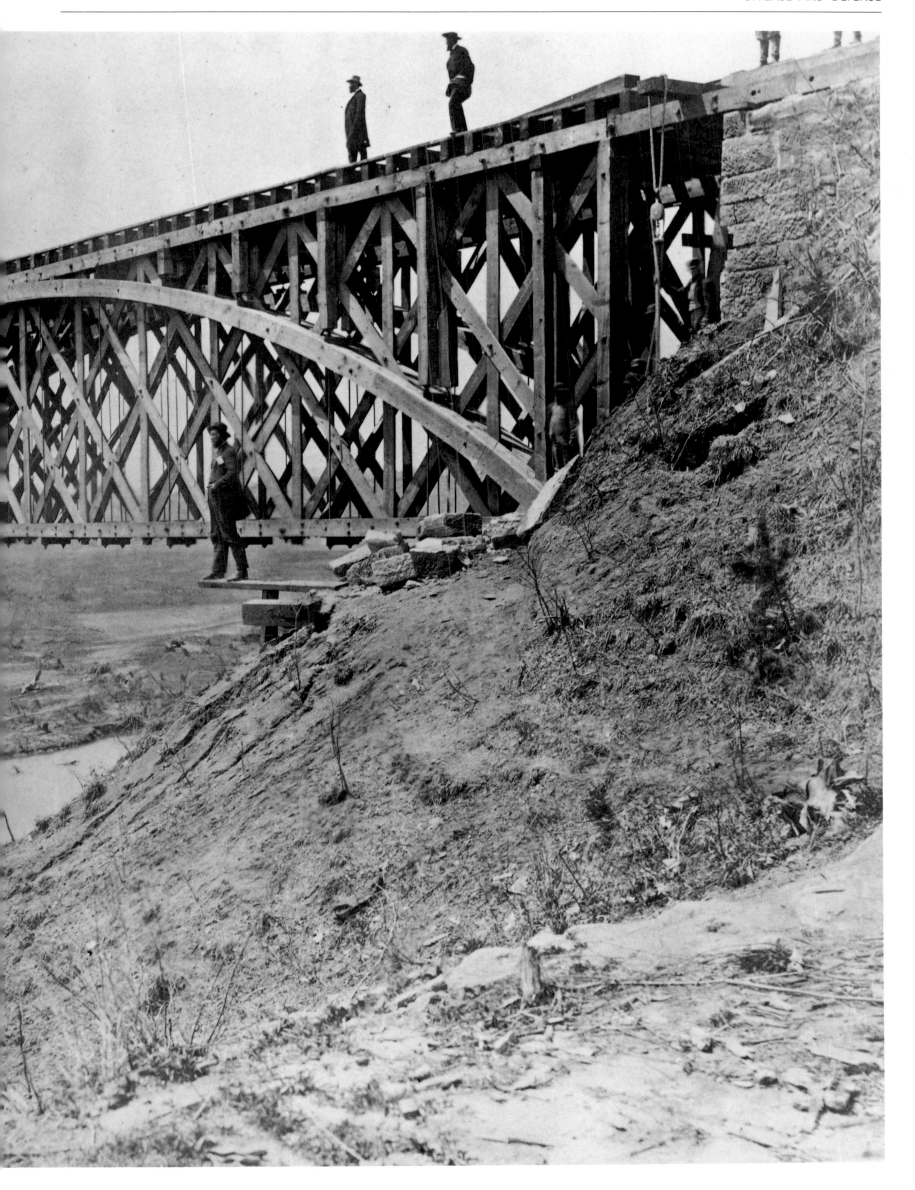

**A Union Construction Corps telegraph station, April 1864,**
Timothy O'Sullivan,
Library of Congress.

**Union engineers constructing the Dutch Gap Canal, August
1864,**
A. J. Russell,
*Chicago Historical Society, Chicago, IL.*

**The Union ironclad *Essex* on the Mississippi, Baton Rouge,
Louisiana, n.d.,**
A. D. Lytle,
*U.S. Army Military History Institute, Carlisle, PA.*

**Confederate defenses in the vicinity of Potter House, Atlanta, Georgia, 1864,**
George Barnard,
*National Archives.*

# PANORAMA AND NARRATIVE

To depict the war in all its complexity, photographers used unusual and innovative camera techniques. The vast, heroic scale of operations was caught in sweeping panoramic views, while some relatively trivial incidents as well as major occurrences were examined in close-up through narrative sequences of images – an exploration of the war in macrocosm and microcosm.

Panoramas, in painted form, dated from a 360° *View of London* (1792) and soon became a popular public entertainment set in special theaters. Later came the moving panorama which was unrolled from one scroll to another, often with accompanying sound and special effects. Of these many primitive travelogues and historical sagas that traversed the United States and Europe from the 1830s on, one of the more famous was John Banvard's *Mississippi* panorama – a three-mile-long canvas that depicted the river for its 1200 miles from the Missouri to New Orleans. Photographers attempted to emulate these spectacles – among them Robert Vance, who produced an 1851 panorama of California scenery in over 300 daguerreotypes, as well as a San Francisco panorama.

Not until late in the 19th century were photographic panoramas taken on a single plate, so Civil War-era panoramas were composed of two or more exposures pieced together. Panoramic effects could be obtained as well on single plate exposures. They ranged from the architectural (Osborn & Durbec's Fort Sumter) and urban (Gardner's views of Richmond) to vistas of encampments and battlefields by Gibson, and urban and landscape views combined, as in Barnard's *Waterfront of Savannah*. The war's most spectacular panoramas were taken by Barnard in a series of multi-plate topographical views from Lookout Mountain as a reference for the mapping of Chattanooga battlefield, as well as in vistas of and around Nashville and Knoxville.

The use of the stereograph camera by O'Sullivan and others made possible, too, narrower panoramas in depth. Most stereo lenses were placed more than 2½ inches apart (the average distance between human eyes) in order to achieve an illusion of exaggerated deep space, or "hyperspace," thus enhancing the visual drama of landscapes. In panoramas, the omniscient viewpoint, objective distance, vast sweep of space and piling up of detail evoked a sense of human control of the environment, and paradoxically, in landscape views conveyed a feeling of meditative and transcendental serenity akin to religious awe.

In a way similar to travel photography, these images allowed those on the homefront to vicariously experience the faraway places named in the news. No matter if the exposure was not perfect: the blurring and "ghosts" left by the motion of people, vehicles, tree leaves in a breeze and water flowing over a dam only added to the realism and authenticity of the photograph. The panoramic and scenic views, in general, of the war years were a prologue for the golden age of American landscape photography to follow. The ever-adaptive Anthonys tacitly acknowledged the aesthetic excellence of many of these pictures by repackaging them as a "Southern Views" series when Civil War photographs failed to draw an audience after 1865.

In technique, panoramic photography was similar to narrative work in that both required the taking of sequential images. In the panorama they were pieced together to represent space, while in narratives they were meant to be viewed in succession in order to reproduce the passage of time. The notion of narrative sequences was not new to photography, although earlier versions had been literary in content.

Brady & Company's June 1862 series on the inflation and flight of the balloon *Intrepid* was an apt metaphor for this new perspective on the documentation of historic events. The immediacy of O'Sullivan's three 1864 views of General Grant and his staff at Massaponax was outstanding. His use of the stereo camera, with its greater flexibility and speed, allowed exposures almost cinematic in quality. Less condensed series included Gardner's coverage of Lincoln's visit with McClellan at Antietam, and the documentation by various photographers of both Lincoln inaugurations. Less consequential series were produced by Russell on the Dutch Gap Canal construction and by San Francisco's Lawrence & Houseworth on the 1864 assembly of the ironclad ship *Camanche*.

In May 1865 many cameramen, including Russell and Gardner and his men, photographed the epic two-day Washington, D.C. victory parade of the Union armies, the Grand Review, before the soldiers were mustered out of service. Gardner concluded his coverage by making formal studio group portraits of Generals Sherman, Grant and Meade, along with their staffs.

The birth of modern photojournalism came with Gardner's series on the capture, trial and execution of Lincoln's assassins (as well as with his later series on the execution of Andersonville prison commandant Henry Wirz). His coverage, assisted by O'Sullivan, included views of key sites such as Ford's Theater, the telegraph office, the livery stable, the bridge across which Booth escaped, and the prison; first, copies of existing portraits of the suspects and later an extensive series on them as prisoners; portraits of their captors, the trial court and hangmen; Booth's autopsy; and finally the execution itself in a series of vivid images.

**General Grant and Staff at Massaponax Church, May 21, 1864,**
Timothy O'Sullivan,
*Library of Congress.*

**Inflating the observation balloon** *Intrepid*, **June 1, 1862,**
Brady & Company,
*Library of Congress.*

**The Union Observation Corps balloon *Intrepid* at Fair Oaks,
June 1, 1862,**
Brady & Company,
*Library of Congress.*

**Thaddeus Lowe (seated, foreground) prepares a telegraph
report based on observation from a Union balloon, n.d.,**
Brady & Company,
*The Bettmann Archive.*

**President Abraham Lincoln meets with General George
McClellan at Antietam, Maryland, October 1862,**
Alexander Gardner,
*Library of Congress.*

**President Abraham Lincoln with General George McClellan and other Union officers at Antietam, Maryland, October 1862,** Alexander Gardner, *National Archives.*

**The execution of four of the Lincoln conspirators, the Old
Penitentiary, Washington, D.C., July 7, 1865,**
Alexander Gardner,
*The Bettmann Archive.*

**The execution of Captain Henry Wirz, November 1865,**
Alexander Gardner,
*Library of Congress.*

**A stereoscopic view of the headquarters of the 5th Corps, Army
of the Potomac, at Spotsylvania, Virginia, May 19, 1864,**
Timothy O'Sullivan,
*Library of Congress.*

TOP: **A panoramic view of the outer walls of Fort Sumter, Charleston Harbor, South Carolina, April 17, 1861,**
Osborn & Durbec,
*Library of Congress.*

ABOVE: **A panoramic view of an Army of the Potomac encampment at Cumberland Landing on the Pamunkey River, May 1862,**
James Gibson,
*Library of Congress.*

**The ruins of Richmond, Virginia, April 6, 1865, (right side of panorama),**
Alexander Gardner,
*U.S. Army Military History Institute, Carlisle, PA.*

**Union engineers constructing a road near the Jericho Mill,
North Anna River, May 1864,**
Timothy O'Sullivan,
*Library of Congress.*

**The waterfront of Savannah,
Georgia, November 1864,**
George Barnard,
*Library of Congress.*

# AFTERMATH

The Civil War's most powerful and haunting photographs were those that inventoried the devastation wreaked on living flesh, the countryside, structures and machines, and on entire cities. Not since Goya's series of etchings, *The Disasters of War*, had the romantic vision of war as a glorious adventure been disputed so effectively. But while Goya's *Disasters* were not published in his lifetime, some of the Civil War's more horrific images reached the public while the conflict was still in progress.

The 95 or so images of Antietam captured by Gardner with Gibson's assistance in September 1862 were, in their exposure of corpses, unlike anything seen before. Realizing their revolutionary nature, Gardner and Gibson copyrighted their views but their names, appearing in fine print on the card mounts, were lost next to Brady's large logo. Response to this shocking chronicle was overwhelming as crowds thronged into Brady's New York gallery to pore over and purchase these photographs.

In July 1863 at Gettysburg, the now independent Gardner, along with Gibson and O'Sullivan, was no longer alone on the field. In competition with Brady & Company as well as Tyson Brothers and others, he vied to produce the most dramatic views. The use of stereo made them even more realistic but realism here, as always, was a relative term. With an eye to composition and message, in some cases Gardner and his men moved bodies around, posed them and used the same rifle as a prop in different scenes. (They probably did not go so far as to pose live soldiers as corpses, though this was done by an unidentified photographer on at least one occasion.) The prime example, *Home of a Rebel Sharpshooter*, taken by and attributed to O'Sullivan in Gardner's 1863 catalog, was published under Gardner's name when included in his 1866 *Sketchbook*.

Gradually the public became less sensitive to such images as further coverage of combat dead followed. In May 1863, Russell photographed bodies along a stone wall at Mayre's Heights, while in May 1864 Brady men detailed the burial of dead at Fredericksburg and O'Sullivan covered a similar operation after the Battle of Spotsylvania. In 1865 a lesser known but more grimly realistic series of 22 stereo views was completed by Roche of Confederate dead in muddy rain-soaked trenches at Fort Mahone, also known as "Fort Damnation." At war's end, perhaps only the atrocity photos of emaciated and skeletal Union prisoners of war from Andersonville evoked a response as strong as Antietam.

As Eisenhower said nearly a century later, "Public opinion wins wars." In the pursuit of war at the psychological level, these images indicted the Confederacy, which was seen as too uncivilized to bury its own dead. Occupying the moral high ground in its opposition to slavery, the Union made effective propaganda use of photographs to demonstrate that the enemy was mortal and hence conquerable, and that the cruelties inflicted on Union prisoners merited a swift retribution.

This exploitation of photographs intentionally skirted the implicit ambiguities. The conditions that contributed to the starvation of Union prisoners of war were created, in no small part, by the Union blockade strangling the South's economy. And for the defeated hastily retiring from the battlefield, it is not always possible to bury one's dead. It is then left to the victor to do so, but only after he has attended to his own fallen heroes.

These images carried as well a broader message on a more universal level. Many of the best photographs of the Civil War's aftermath have been transformed over the passage of time into symbolic icons of the brutality and futility of war. For the citizens of the time, who no longer cared to see them, these photographs were probably of little assistance in completing what Freud called the "work of mourning." But for the generations that follow, they offer up a complex melange of motifs and metaphors about the transience of life, the enigma of death, and the decay of civilizations.

One of the most arresting pictures was that taken by Gardner of the dead horse at Antietam. In its strangely life-like posture the horse attracted the attention of other battlefield visitors, including Oliver Wendell Holmes, who had come to search for his missing son, the future Supreme Court justice. Today the horse resonates with apocalyptic significance – "And I looked, and behold a pale horse: and his name that sat on him was Death, and Hell followed with him." And the views of architectural ruins did not just document the destruction of the enemy's infrastructure and industrial capacity – flour mills, in particular, allowed the Confederate Army to endure – they also offered a touchstone for meditation on matters of a more cosmic nature.

In the landscape and architecture photos taken as he followed Sherman through the South and later presented in his book, *Photographic Views* Barnard was especially attentive to their aesthetic and symbolic aspects. (In order to increase the picturesqueness of a scene, he was not above adding clouds from a second negative.) Barnard's views of the ruins of Atlanta, Columbia and Charleston, as well as the views of Richmond by Gardner and others, conveyed a symbolism well understood in its day. In 19th century literature and art, architectural ruins from classical times were seen as a moral lesson on the folly of human pride and selfishness, which inevitably led to the corruption and extinction of these ancient cultures – an obvious parallel to the Civil War years.

**The interior of Fort Sumter, Charleston Harbor, South Carolina, after a Union bombardment, September 8, 1863,**
George S. Cook,
*Library of Congress.*

**City of Atlanta, 1864,**
George Barnard,
*National Archives.*

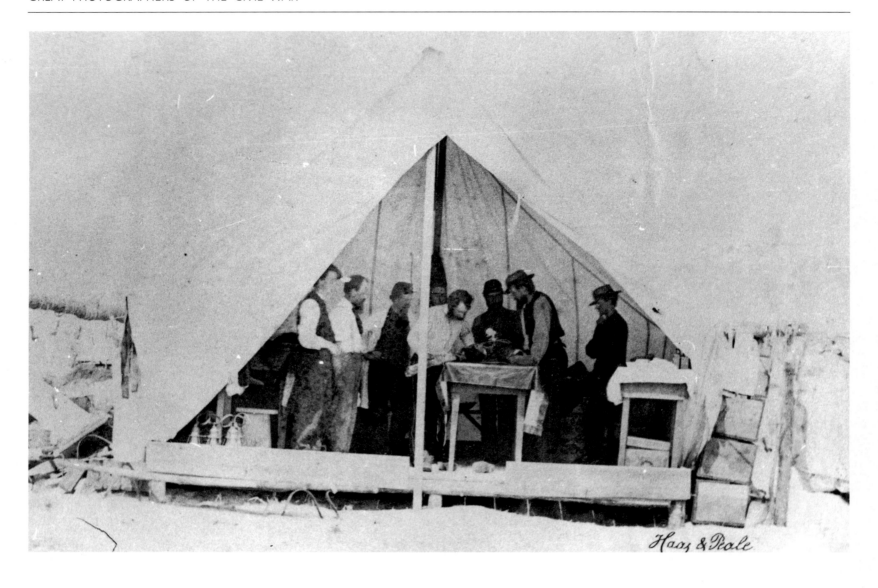

**Surgery on a wounded soldier, Morris Island, South Carolina,**
**July 1863,**
Haas and Peale,
*U.S. Army Military History Institute, Carlisle, PA.*

**Wounded Union Troops on Marye's Heights, Fredericksburg, Virginia, May 1864,**
Brady & Company,
*Museum of the Confederacy, Richmond, VA.*

**Andersonville Prison, Georgia, 1865,**
A. J. Riddle,
*Library of Congress.*

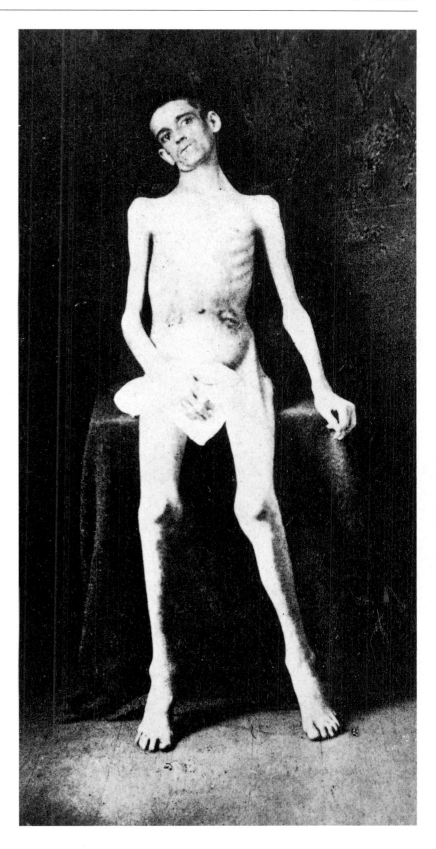

**A Union prisoner after his release from the Confederate prison at Belle Isle, May 1864,**
Brady & Company,
*Library of Congress.*

**Destruction of the
Roundhouse, Atlanta,
Georgia, 1864,**
George Barnard,
*Library of Congress.*

**Ruins of the "Car Shed," Atlanta, November 1864,**
George Barnard,
*Library of Congress.*

**The burnt-out remains of the Gallego Flour Mills, Richmond,
Virginia, April 1865,**
Alexander Gardner,
*U.S. Army Military History Institute, Carlisle, PA.*

**Burial party, Cold Harbor, Virginia, April 1865,**
John Reekie,
*Library of Congress.*

**"Home of a Rebel Sharpshooter,"** Gettysburg, 1863,
Timothy O'Sullivan,
*Chicago Historical Society, Chicago, IL.*

**A Union casualty station at Savage Station, Virginia, after the Battle of Fair Oaks, June 1862,**
James Gibson,
*Library of Congress.*

**General Haupt, at left, surveying the damage to an artillery
battery's animals and equipment, after the Battle of
Chancellorsville, May 1863,**
A. J. Russell,
*Library of Congress.*

**View from the Soldiers National Cemetery, Gettysburg, July 4,
1865,**
Alexander Gardner,
*Library of Congress.*

**"Harvest of Death," Gettysburg, 1863,**
Timothy O'Sullivan,
*Chicago Historical Society, Chicago, IL.*

**The ruins of Columbia, South Carolina, after its capture by
Sherman, 1865,**
George Barnard,
*Library of Congress.*

**The ruins of the Norfolk Naval Yard, Virginia, December 1864**,
James Gardner,
*National Archives.*

**Confederate dead at the foot
of Marye's Heights,
Fredericksburg, Virginia, after
the successful assault by the
6th Maine Infantry Regiment,
May 3, 1863,**
A. J. Russell,
*Library of Congress.*

**Confederate dead in Bloody Lane, Antietam, September 19, 1862,**
Alexander Gardner,
*Chicago Historical Society, Chicago, IL.*

**Destruction of Hood's ordnance train, Atlanta, Georgia, 1864,**
George Barnard,
*Library of Congress.*

**Manassas Junction, Virginia,
after its evacuation by
Confederate forces, 1862,**
George Barnard,
*Library of Congress.*

# ACKNOWLEDGMENTS

The author and publisher would like to thank Design 23, the designers; Stephen Small, the editor; Rita Longabucco for the picture research; Veronica Price and Nicki Giles for production; and the following agencies and institutions for providing the photographs:

**American Antiquarian Society, Worcester, MA, pages:** 12(bottom)

**The Bettmann Archive, pages:** 1, 43, 70, 74-5

**Chicago Historical Society, pages:** 7, 21, 41, 53, 63, 99, 103, 108

**Confederate Memorial Hall, New Orleans, LA, pages:** 6

**Florida State Archives, Tallahassee, FL, pages:** 40

**Collection of the J. Paul Getty Museum, Malibu, CA, pages:** 34

**Library of Congress, pages:** 5, 8, 9, 12(top), 14(both), 18, 19(top), 22, 23, 35, 36-7, 38, 39, 42, 44-5, 49, 51, 52, 57, 58, 60-1, 62, 67, 68, 69, 71, 76, 77, 80-1(both), 83, 84-5, 87, 92, 93, 94-5, 96, 98, 100, 101, 102, 104, 107, 109, 110

**Museum of the Confederacy, Richmond, VA, pages:** 91

**National Archives, pages:** 2, 20, 25, 28-9, 50, 54-5, 65, 72-3, 88-9, 105-6

**New Hampshire Historical Society, Concord, NH, pages:** 17, 32, 33, 56

**National Army Museum, London, England, pages:** 10, 11

**Otto G. Richter Library, University of Miami, pages:** 13

**U.S. Army Military History Institute, Carlisle, PA, pages:** 16(both), 19(bottom), 26, 27, 30-1, 64, 82, 90, 97

**Southern Historical Collection, The University of North Carolina, Chapel Hill, NC, pages:** 59

**U.S. Military Academy Library, West Point, NY, pages:** 15